Media chemistry

Exploring the elements of online communication

Clive Shepherd

onlignment

ISBN: 978-1-4466-1951-3

First published in 2011

http://www.onlignment.com/

Exploring the elements of online communication

All online communication, whether that's published content, live online events or social media, make use of the same key media elements: text, audio, images, animation and video.

The online communicator needs to know when to use each of these elements, how to do so effectively within the particular constraints associated with working online, and how best to combine media elements to achieve their communications objectives. This resource has been prepared to shed some light on these issues and to encourage more rewarding online communication for all involved.

onlignment

1

Text as a media element

1

Text as a media element

What text is good for

Text is by far the most flexible and pervasive of all the media elements. When carefully composed, it is capable of conveying precise meaning.

In most circumstances (where it not integrated into a video or animation), text can be absorbed at the reader's own pace, which reduces the stress for the reader in a learning context and makes it much easier for those who want to skim content or hunt down a particular piece of information.

When text is not so suitable

Text is not as expressive as speech, because it does not convey tone of voice. For this reason, text messages can be easily misinterpreted.

Without considerable skill on the part of the author, text is not great at describing the physical appearance of an object or person (use photos or illustrations instead), actual events (use video), layouts (use diagrams or screen grabs in the case of software), or complex processes (use diagrams or animations). Text is also not ideal for describing sounds (use audio!).

In most cases, text is less suitable than audio as an accompaniment for dynamic visual media such as video, animations, software simulations, slide shows and live application sharing sessions.

Optimising text for online delivery

Text is harder to read from a screen than it is from paper, partly because the resolution of the screen is so much lower (less dots per character) and also because the light is projected rather than reflected. With scrolling and paging, it is also much easier for the reader to lose their orientation within an online document.

With these points in mind, best practice suggests that you:

- Limit your word count to half of what it would be in print.

- Use clear, descriptive headings to separate sections.

- Keep sentences short.

- Cover only a single point in each paragraph.

- Use bulleted or numbered lists rather than present a series of related items as ordinary prose.

Be aware that, for the visually impaired, on-screen text can be read aloud by screen readers. To help screen readers work at their best, text should be formatted and displayed in accordance with the latest accessibility guidelines. In most cases this will be an issue for the person setting up the website rather than the author.

Combining text with other elements

As a verbal element, text combines well with visual elements but clashes badly with a second verbal element such as speech. So, text plus still images works well, whereas text plus speech causes all sorts of confusion and overload for the user.

The brain cannot process two verbal inputs simultaneously, so the user has to block out one element (usually the speech because this is conveyed much more slowly than text) in order to concentrate on the other.

How text is represented online

Text is represented digitally as individual ASCII characters of one byte each. For this reason, text is by far the most bandwidth-friendly element.

Portions of a piece of text can be emboldened, italicised or underlined. As a general rule, underlining should be avoided as it implies that the text is a selectable hyperlink.

Text can also be formatted in terms of point size, colour, font, spacing, column width and alignment, although these aspects of typography are now more normally handled through what is called a 'cascading style sheet' (CSS). This is set up by a designer, leaving the author to worry about the content.

Typography has an important impact on legibility and usability and so determines much more than the style.

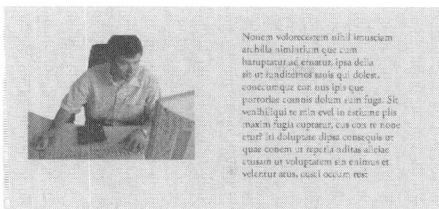

Text provides an ideal accompaniment for a still image

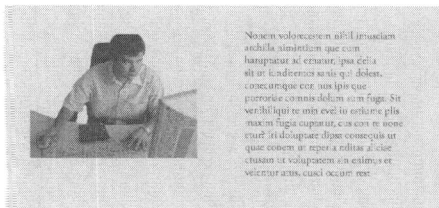

.. but if speech is added as well, then the combination of two verbal sources is confusing for the user.

The following general pointers will help:

* Constrain column width to 5" (12cm) to reduce the eye strain involved in tracking back to the start of each new line.

* Left align paragraphs in most circumstances.

* Limit the use of text that is all capitals.

* Present body text at 10 or 12 point.

* Maintain a high contrast between text and background. In most cases, black on white is fine.

* Use fonts that are optimised for the screen.

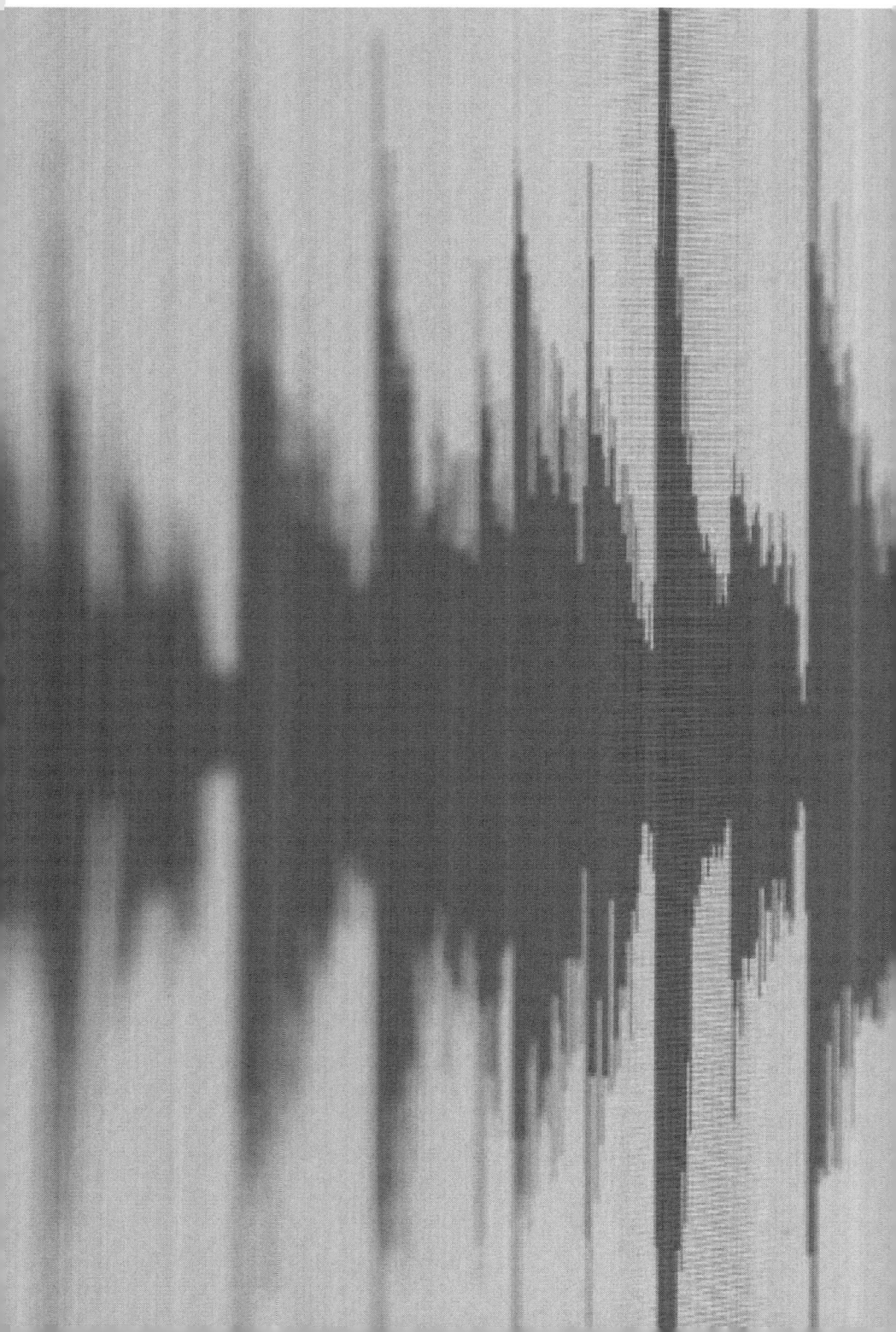

2

Audio as a media element

2

Audio as a media element

What audio is good for

To rather state the obvious, audio is useful when we want to know what something sounds like - a human voice, a piece of music, a fire alarm, a bird song. In these situations, textual descriptions will always be second best.

More commonly, we use sound as an alternative verbal channel to text. In fact, it's a very rich alternative because it conveys tone of voice as well as the words.

In an online context, audio is useful because it takes up no space on the screen. When you're presenting a sequence of images, an animation, a software demonstration or a movie, the verbal content of your message can be delivered in sound without taking attention away from the visual elements.

Audio requires much more in terms of technical paraphernalia.

Although not so often a key factor in online communication, music has the capacity to alter mood more successfully than any other medium.

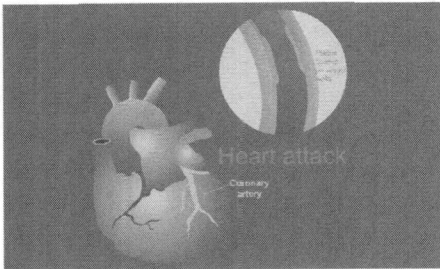

Audio takes up no space on the screen, allowing the user to maintain visual focus on the graphical content.

When audio is not so suitable

Unlike text, audio is not self-paced. Although the user may have the facility to rewind and fast forward recorded audio, they cannot control the speed at which the sound is delivered; and with a live audio stream, even this capability is lost.

Delivery of the spoken word is much slower than the speed at which a person can read, which might, in some circumstances, frustrate a user from achieving their goal as quickly as they would like.

Audio also requires more in terms of technical paraphernalia. The listener needs a sound card and either speakers or headphones; and in a live online conversation, the contributors also need microphones. In an open office environment, there is the additional risk of causing disturbance to those working nearby.

It goes without saying that sound will be inadequate when the subject matter is highly visual or is better understood with visual aids. In these situations audio can be combined with, or replaced entirely by photos, illustrations, video, diagrams, screen grabs or animations. Audio-only media, such as podcasts, will clearly struggle when a visual element is required to convey the intended meaning.

Optimising audio for online delivery

If your audio is pre-recorded and intended for *download* by the user (that's when they wait while the file is saved in full to their computer, but can then play it repeatedly offline), then it pays to minimise the file size by keeping the duration of the audio short. A good example is with podcasts - better to distribute your programme in three 5MB sections rather than one of 15MB. This constraint does not apply

Interviews and discussions make much more engaging listening than monologues.

when the audio is *streamed* (that's when the audio plays almost immediately but is not stored on the user's computer), as will be the case with live audio or when the audio forms part of a multimedia presentation.

Generally speaking, it pays to limit the user's exposure to a single voice. However interesting the speaker and however expressive the voice, any listener will begin to tune out after 10 minutes or so. On radio, you will rarely hear a single voice continuously for more than a minute or two. For this reason, interviews, discussions, question and answer sessions and drama work much better than monologues.

In *The Media Equation*, Stanford University researchers Byron Reeves and Clifford Nass reported on the impact that audio quality had on a user's overall impression of their media experience. Their conclusion was that audio quality *does* matter a great deal, which is an argument for taking care when recording and editing, and then sampling at the best rate possible given the bandwidth constraints.

It pays to use a quality microphone, ideally with a pop shield fitted, as above. The speaker should be 4-5" away from the microphone.

When recording it pays to use quality microphones (ideally fitted with pop shields, which reduce the explosive peaks that occur when speakers say the letter 'p'). Ideally the room will be free of reflections (so few natural reverberations or echoes) and the speaker should be a comfortable distance (say four or five inches) from the microphone. The recording level should be high enough to avoid background hiss, while avoiding the high peaks that cause 'clipping'. When editing, bad takes and gaps can be removed and the overall volume level equalised using a process called 'compression'.

If you are recording a narration to accompany a multimedia presentation or an e-learning programme, it pays to employ a professional voiceover artist. While this may appear to be extravagant, the cost rarely exceeds a few hundred dollars and can make a big difference to the professionalism of the end result.

Audio can be captured on a portable recording device (a digital recorder, a phone or camera) or directly into a computer. In the case of the latter, it pays to work with dedicated audio software if you can, as this will provide you with much more flexibility when it comes to editing (although professional audio editors are expensive, free software such as Audacity is good enough for most purposes). On the other hand, many authoring tools allow you to record directly into the tool and, with a little care, the results can be more than adequate.

 To accommodate those users who have a hearing impairment, you need to provide a transcript of any important audio components within recorded media.

Combining audio with other elements

As a verbal element, speech combines well with visual elements but clashes badly with a second verbal element such as text. So, audio over a sequence of images works well, whereas if the words are replicated on the screen as text, the user stands to be confused and frustrated. The brain cannot process two verbal inputs simultaneously, so the most likely consequence is that the user will reach for the volume control to block out the slower of the two verbal sources, the speech. Of course, if the content of the audio is music or sound effects, this will not clash with the text and can work well.

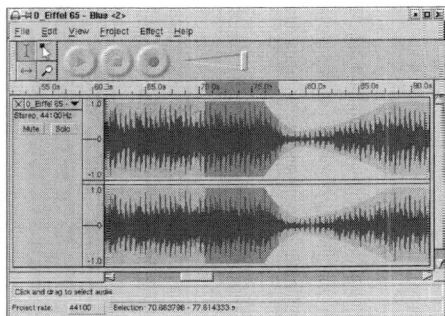

Dedicated audio software, such as Audacity, will provide you with the greatest flexibility when it comes to editing.

How audio is represented online

Digital audio is represented as a stream of 'samples'. The quality of these samples is determined by the frequency with which the samples are taken (the more often the better) and the resolution of the samples (the more bits used to describe each sample the better). As an example, CD audio is sampled 48,100 times per second (48.1KHz) with a 16 bit resolution. Typically, much lower sample qualities are used online in order to reduce the strain on bandwidth (the speed with which data can be transmitted across the network). Most music is recorded as two-channels of samples (stereo), whereas a single channel (mono) is acceptable in many circumstances and certainly when the content is simple speech.

Even when the audio is encoded in mono and at a lower sample quality, it will still be far too bulky to download or stream without extensive compression. The most common compression formats are:

• MP3

• AAC (Apple's alternative to MP3)

• WMA (Windows Media Audio)

Most audio editing software will be able to export in a wide variety of compression formats.

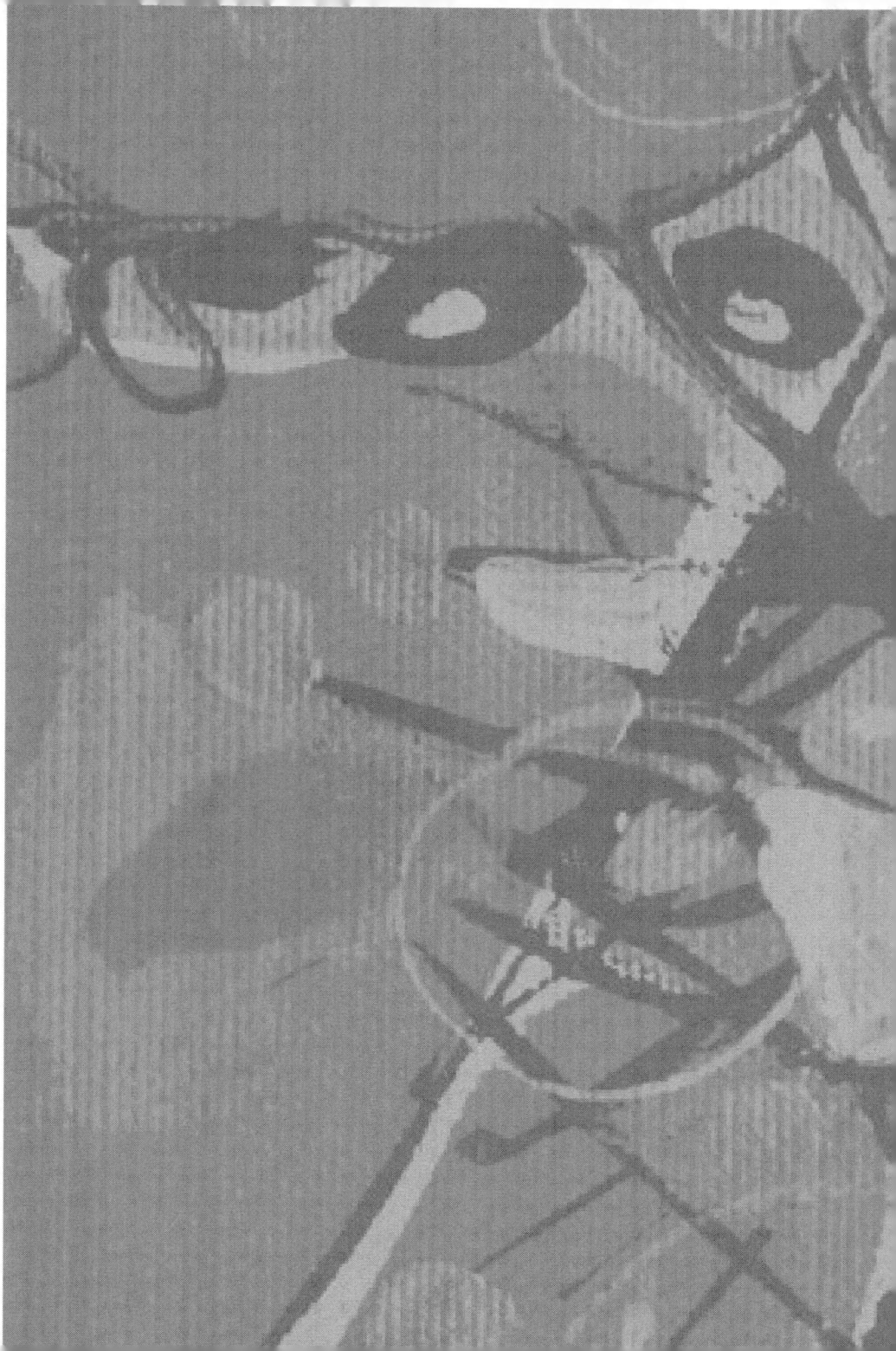

3

The image as a media element

3

The image as a media element

What images are good for

Imagine how difficult it would be to convey the following without the aid of images:

- The new office that we will all be moving to later this year.
- Sales territories in the Indian sub-continent.
- Welcome to our new head of HR.
- The process to follow when troubleshooting a machine breakdown.
- Our fall fashion collection.
- The process of condensation.
- The workings of the internal combustion engine.
- Comparative sales figures over the past five years.
- The cypress tree.
- The structure of the Internet backbone.

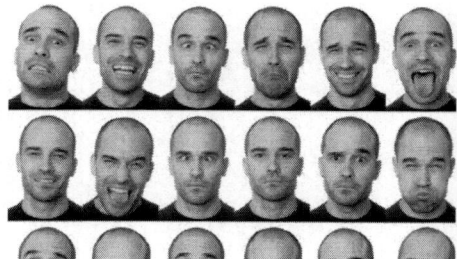

Charts, illustrations, diagrams and photographs make it possible to describe relationships, trends, structures, likenesses and much more in ways that words can not.

Images come in a variety of forms and these all have their particular place:

- *Photographs* are capable of accurately depicting real-life people, objects, places and events.

- *Illustrations*, including clip-art and cartoons, will not capture people, objects, places and events as faithfully as photos, but can depict what is impossible or impractical to photograph. In their relative simplicity, they may also communicate more clearly than photos.

- *Diagrams* illustrate cause and effect relationships and the relationships between the parts of something and the whole. They include timelines, organagrams, maps and flow charts.

- *Charts* provide a rapidly-accessible visual representation of numerical data, highlighting trends and proportions.

- *Screen shots* faithfully capture the elements of a software interface.

When images are not so suitable

As a general rule, images struggle to convey precise meaning without verbal support from either speech or text; and it goes without saying that they have little practical function when there is no strong visual aspect to the content.

Still images will be second best to animation or video when communicating movement or representing live action.

When used for purely decorative purposes, images use up valuable bandwidth and screen space without adding anything to the communication process.

Optimising images for online delivery

When displayed online, images need to be large enough to be clear but not so large as to require excessive scrolling.

Copyright laws apply as much online as in any other medium

The screen is not the ideal setting for highly detailed images because of the limited resolution of most screens, typically less than 100 dots per inch. Compare this with print, where resolutions start at 300 dpi and can be very much higher. As a general rule, highly detailed images are better made available for download or delivered in hard copy format.

Copyright laws apply as much online as in any other medium. If you use copyrighted images in your online communications without permission, then you are taking a risk.

If the images you intend to use are not your own property, then look for images which are copyright cleared or which are covered by a Creative Commons license.

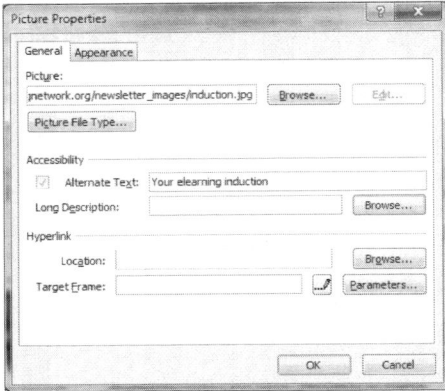

Any web editor or content management system will allow you to enter alternate text which can be read aloud to visually-impaired users by screen reader software.

Accessibility guidelines dictate that, when you use images online, you provide each image with an alternative textual description. This allows those users with a visual impairment to gain some benefit from your images, because screen readers can convert your descriptions into synthesised speech.

Combining images with other elements

Images combine well with audio or text. With audio, you have the advantage that the eye can concentrate on the image, while the verbal content is communicated aurally; with text, on the other hand, the eye has to switch back and forth.

Images do not combine well with a second visual source such as live video. If you want the user to focus on the image, then it's best to turn the video off, at least temporarily.

How images are represented online

Online images can be held in one of a number of compressed, bit-mapped formats. With bit-mapping, the images are stored digitally as a data structure representing a rectangular grid of pixels. Each pixel in this grid is represented by a colour or greyscale value.

Bit-mapped images can be contrasted with vector graphics, which describe the image as a series of geometric functions (lines, curves, etc.). Vector graphics have the advantage of being more scalable, retaining their quality however large they are displayed. Most images other than photographs are created and edited in vector format, but must be exported as a compressed bit-map for use online.

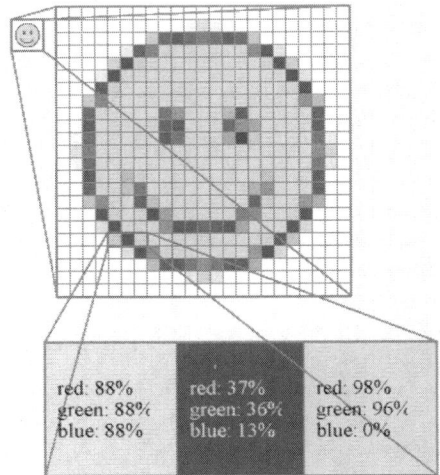

This enlarged bit-map shows how the image is stored as a rectangular grid of pixels, each with a specific colour, defined as a combination of red, green and blue.

Because this removes the ability for high-quality scaling, it makes sense to export the images at the maximum size at which they will be displayed online. If you leave it to the browser to do the up-scaling, be prepared to lose a lot of quality.

When delivering images online, you have three choices of bit-mapped image formats:

- **JPEG** (Joint Photographic Experts Group) - pronounced 'jaypeg' and sometimes shortened to just JPG. This format is 'lossy' in that the more you compress the image and thus reduce file size, the greater you will lose clarity and detail. JPEG graphics can render in full colour and are ideally suited to the display of photographs.

- **GIF** (Graphics Interchange Format) is 'lossless' in that the compression process does not involve sacrificing quality. GIF graphics are limited to 256 colours, which is fine for computer graphics with hard edges and block colours, but not so good for photos. They can also have a transparent background, which can be useful if you want to display your images in anything other than a simple rectangular arrangement.

- **PNG** (Portable Network Graphics) - pronounced 'ping' - is another 'lossless' format but is not restricted in colour rendition, making it a superior format to GIF. PNGs are ideal for computer-generated graphics such as buttons, logos, diagrams and maps, but are less suited to photographs, where the resulting file size is likely to be excessive. Be a little careful, because not all online applications - or corporate firewalls - support PNG.

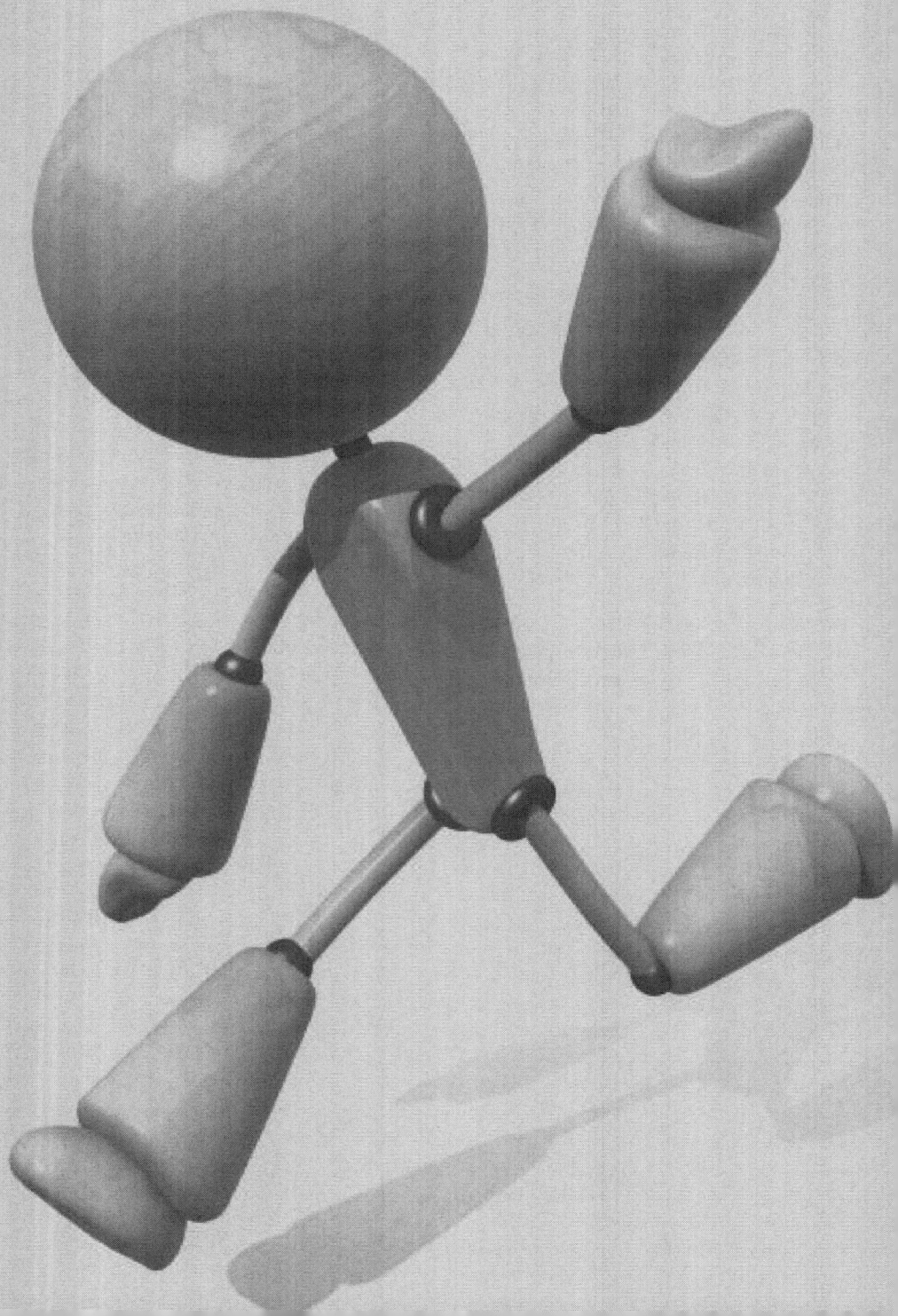

4

Animation as a media element

4

Animation as a media element

What animation is good for

Animation is to diagrams and illustrations what video is to photographs. The added ingredient in each case is motion, and motion can be useful: it is eye-catching; it can represent in simplified form the action that we experience in real-life; it can also help in explaining how elements interact with each other.

Online animations come in a variety of forms:

- *Transitions* provide a bridge from one state to another, usually just for decorative purposes.

- *Animated diagrams* are particularly useful when explaining how things work and what the stages are in a process.

- *Animated cartoons* function as they always have, as entertainment.

- *Interactive games and simulations* have the potential to engage users in motivating challenges, free of risk.

- *Software sims* explain how tasks are completed in software packages.

- *3D environments* go beyond the 2D to provide a more immersive experience, whether for gaming or for interaction in real-time with other online users.

- *Application and desktop sharing*, as used by web conferencing and other online communication tools, make it possible to review what is on a person's computer from a remote location.

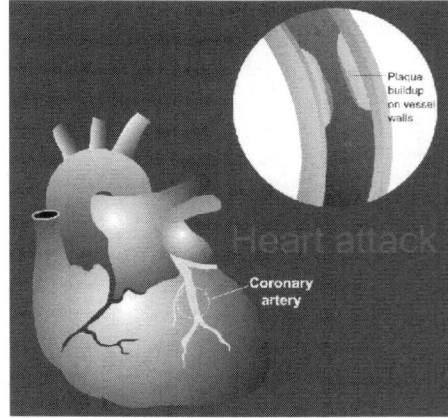

Animated diagrams are useful for explaining how things work, in this case a heart attack.

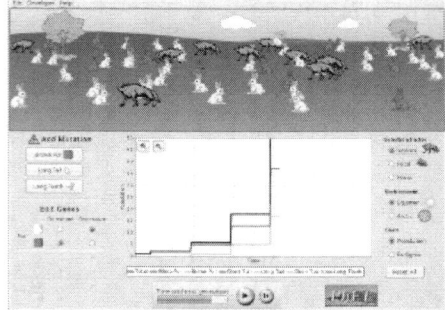

Interactive simulations allow users to explore cause and effect relationships, as in this simulation of natural selection, created by the University of Colorado at Boulder.

When animation is not so suitable

Animations, like images, struggle to convey precise meaning without verbal support from either speech or text. And they clearly have little practical function when there is no strong visual aspect to the content.

When used purely as an attention grabber, animations can be annoyingly distracting. Users have been known to cover up a repetitive animation with their hand so they can concentrate on a task elsewhere on the screen.

Optimising animations for online delivery

As a general rule, animation should be used only very modestly for decoration or show. If a user is engaging with an online experience primarily for their own amusement or entertainment then fine, but more often than not the user is goal-orientated and does not want any distractions that get in the way of achieving that goal. A good example is the way in which elaborate animations are sometimes used to provide a gateway into a site - more often than not, users will find this annoying and look to get past it as quickly as possible. Online, the need is for speed; to get to the point.

Where animation is the main feature, as it would be with an animated cartoon or a software sim, then it makes sense to organise the content into short modules which users can access easily from a menu. You'll also need to make it easy for users to replay any animation.

If you're using an animation to draw attention to something new or important, then don't loop endlessly, because this becomes irritating and distracting.

Combining animation with other elements

Animations combine particularly well with audio, which allows the eye to maintain attention on the animation, while the verbal content is communicated aurally. Text is an option, but then the eye has to switch back and forth.

Animations do not combine well with a second visual source such as live video. If you want the user to focus on the animation, then it's best to turn the video off, at least temporarily.

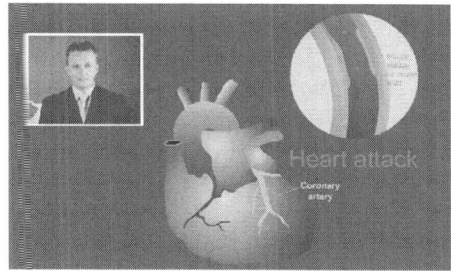

Here the presenter talking to camera distracts the user from the animation, which in this case should be the user's visual focus of attention.

How animations are represented online

In the early days of the World Wide Web, the only available animation format was the 'animated GIF'. This allows a series of images in the GIF format to be sequenced and looped. Animated GIFs are still used, notably for advertising banners, but the format is too bulky and inflexible for any serious animation tasks.

```
<script type="text/javascript">
function starttimer()
{
 d=new Date()
 for (count=0;count<imagemax;count++)
 {
  yyy = yp[count]*Math.cos(rx)-
zp[count]*Math.sin(rx);
  bbb = bp[count]*Math.cos(rx)-
cp[count]*Math.sin(rx);
  zzz = yp[count]*Math.
sin(rx)+zp[count]*Math.cos(rx);
  ccc = bp[count]*Math.
sin(rx)+cp[count]*Math.cos(rx);
  xxx = xp[count]*Math.cos(ry)+zzz*Math.
sin(ry);
  aaa = ap[count]*Math.cos(ry)+ccc*Math.
sin(ry);
  zzz = xp[count]*-Math.sin(ry)+zzz*Math.
cos(ry);
  ccc = ap[count]*-Math.sin(ry)+ccc*Math.
cos(ry);
          // PERSPECTIVE
        xxx=xxx*(perspective/
(zzz+perspective));
        yyy=yyy*(perspective/
(zzz+perspective));
        aaa=aaa*(perspective/
(ccc+perspective));
        bbb=bbb*(perspective/
(ccc+perspective));

  line(image[count],320+xxx,240+yyy,320+aaa,
240+bbb)
 }
 ry-=(mouse_x-320)/5000
 rx+=(mouse_y-240)/5000
 timer=setTimeout("starttimer()",10)
}
function stoptimer()
{
```

Animations can be created using programming languages, such as JavaScript above, but to do so requires the specialist expertise of a web programmer.

Later versions of HTML and JavaScript (the formatting and scripting languages supported by al web browsers) have evolved such that there are now quite a few ways to build transitions, animated buttons and drag and drop facilities into standard web pages, without recourse to third-party plug-ins. However, these facilities require expert coding and are still not adequate for more advanced purposes.

Macromedia introduced the Flash format in 1996 as a way of adding animation capabilities to web pages. Because Flash stores graphical elements in vector format, the animations (saved as Flash 'movies') are small in size and can be scaled up or down without losing quality.

The Flash format has grown enormously in sophistication and popularity since then and, in its current form, now under the wing of Adobe, it is capable of driving complete websites and applications as well as smaller interactive and multimedia elements within standard websites. Artists and designers can work directly with the Flash tool (and its associated scripting language ActionScript) to create bespoke animations, games, simulations and applications. However, the technology is also accessible to less specialist users through much simpler third-party applications which export in the Flash format. Examples include software simulation tools, game engines and many e-learning authoring tools.

Most but not all browsers can run Flash. Where not, this is usually because of the IT policy of a particular organisation, rather than the capability of the computer or browser. It does matter which version of Flash is being used, because earlier versions have much reduced functionality.

Interactive 3D environments are not supported directly on the World Wide Web but some, such as this simulation created using the Thinking Worlds tool, can be displayed using the Adobe Shockwave plug-in.

3D environments are not supported directly within HTML or Flash, although some applications (such as Caspian Learning's *Thinking Worlds* tool) will work in a standard browser with the aid of the Adobe Shockwave plugin. More commonly, 3D games and virtual worlds such as *Second Life* have to be installed on the local computer.

Non-interactive animations, such as cartoons and software sims, can also be rendered as videos. This increases the range of situations in which the animations can be accessed (principally because some mobile devices, notably the iPhone and iPad, do not support Flash), but restricts the ability to scale the animations without quality loss.

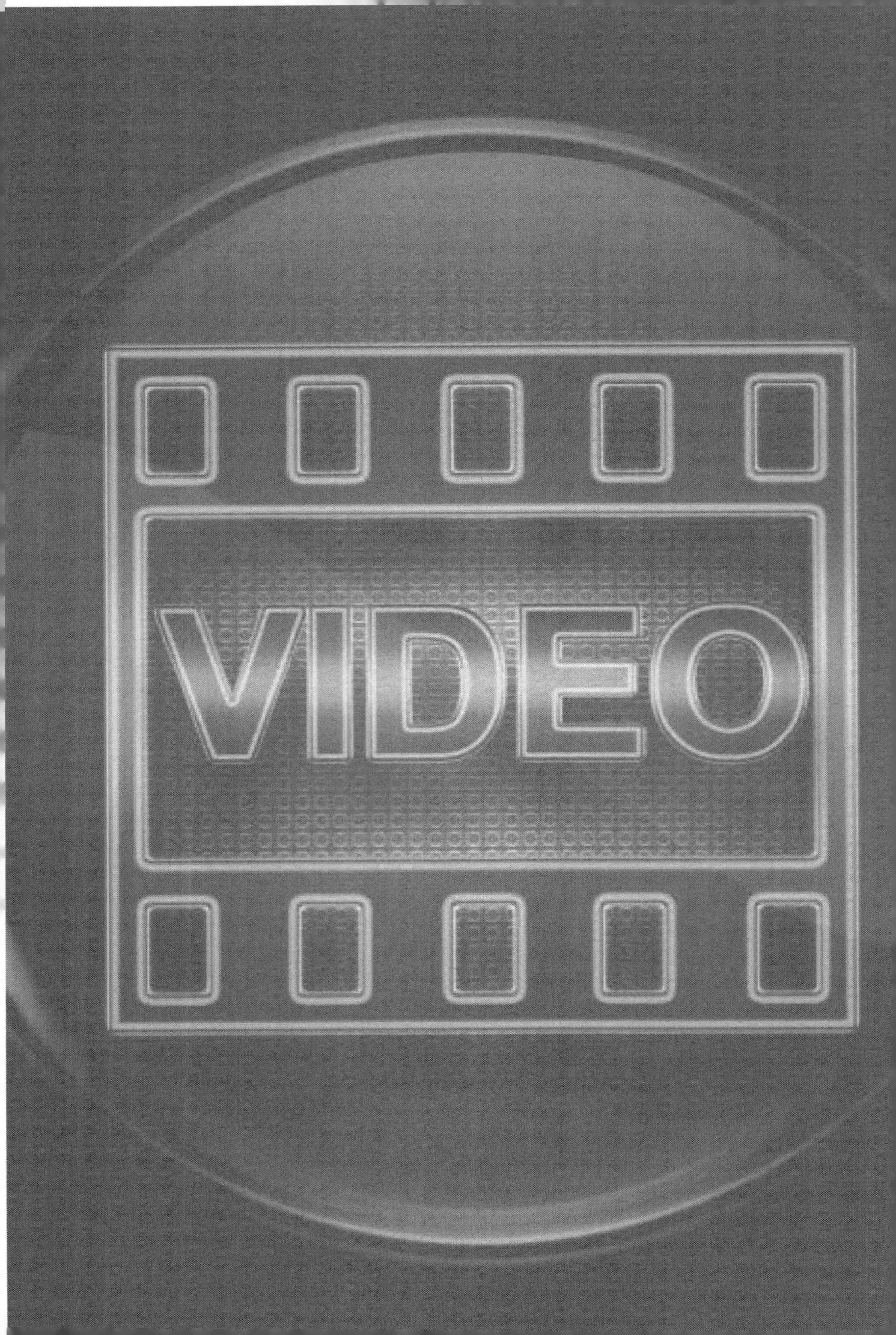
VIDEO

5

Video as a media element

5

Video as a media element

What video is good for

Video excels at depicting real-life events. So, assuming that a particular real-life event is of interest to you, then if it moves and you can point a camera at it, video really is your medium of choice. As another real bonus, it's easy to record audio at the same time in perfect synch, meaning video is really two media elements packaged as one.

Because the visual and audio content of a video is constantly changing, it attracts and maintains attention. Just think how your eye gets drawn to the TV, even with the sound off.

Video is perfect for showing pre-recorded material, but can also be used to deliver live video feeds, through simple webcams or top-end video conferencing services, such as telepresence.

Video can do more than show what a camera can capture; it can also be used as a simple, alternative means for displaying a wide range of other multimedia material, such as software sims, narrated PowerPoint presentations, scenes from virtual worlds or Flash animations.

When video is not so suitable

Video is not self-paced. Although you may have the facility to rewind and fast forward recorded video, you cannot control the speed at which the audio content is

Video can be used for pre-recorded material but is equally valuable for providing a live feed through a webcam or high-end video conferencing system.

delivered; with a live video stream, you have no control at all. Because video is not self-paced, it provides the viewer with less opportunity for reflection or note-taking.

Two-way live video is only feasible when each participant has a webcam integrated within, or connected to, their computer.

Because video is the most bandwidth-hungry of all media elements, users with bandwidth constraints will be unable to take advantage.

Video requires more bandwidth than any other media element. Without adequate bandwidth, video downloads will be frustratingly lengthy and it will not be possible to display live video at an acceptable frame rate.

Clearly video has little to offer when the content is not visual in nature or when there is little movement in the visual content.

Optimising video for online delivery

Because online video is typically displayed in a small window, it works best when the subject matter does not contain a lot of fine detail. In years to come, when bandwidth ceases to be much of an issue, then this constraint will drop away and online high-definition playback will no doubt become commonplace.

With pre-recorded video, it makes sense to organise the content into short modules which users can access easily from a menu. In YouTube, you can organise a collection of modules into a playlist with a single URL.

Video can be captured on a portable recording device (a camcorder, a stills camera with video capability or a phone) or directly into a computer via a webcam. If you are using a webcam to capture your

material, it pays to take a little time to ensure you frame the subject carefully and that the scene is well lit.

Note that, if your material is only ever going to be played back online in a normal window, then there is little to be gained by recording in HD (high definition). Recording in standard definition will dramatically reduce the data size of your recordings and reduce the strain on your computer's processor when editing.

In anything other than live situations, you'll benefit from carrying out some editing of your content. There are free tools such as Microsoft MovieMaker and Apple's iMovie; very capable low-cost versions of professional tools, such as Adobe Premiere Elements; and, of course, the top-end tools themselves, such as Avid, Adobe Premiere and Final Cut Pro. In most cases, the free and low-cost tools are more than adequate

Pre-recorded video is best organised into short modules. In this example, an interview has been divided into a number of short sections, each of which can be easily accessed using a YouTube playlist menu overlay.

Free and low-cost video editing tools such as Apple iMovie are more than adequate for the post-production of video that's intended for delivery online.

for the simple editing required when creating online video.

 Note that, to accommodate those users who have a visual or auditory impairment, you need to provide a transcript of any important video material.

Combining video with other elements

Video obviously combines well with audio, because this allows the eye to concentrate on the visual material, while the verbal content is communicated aurally. It would not work to display text alongside a video;

so, if audio really is not feasible – perhaps because users' computers are not fitted with sound cards – then the text should be superimposed on the video, like sub-titles.

Video does not combine well with another visual source. Whichever element is not the primary focus of attention should be turned off or removed.

How videos are represented online

Video quality is determined by the resolution (the number of pixels making up the image) and the frame rate. As a guide, standard definition TV is displayed at 720x576 / 25 frames per second (fps) in Europe or 720x480 / 30 fps in the USA. High definition has between a two and five times better resolution. Digital audio quality is determined by the sample resolution and frequency and the number of channels (see the section on audio).

Video can be recorded and edited in a wide range of digital formats, but will require extensive compression before it is suitable for online delivery. The most common file formats for online video distribution are:

- **MP4** (MPEG-4 / H.264) - the user must have Adobe Flash or Apple QuickTime installed.

- **FLV** (Flash video) - the user must have Adobe Flash installed.

- **WMV** (Windows Media Video) - the user must have Windows Media Player installed.

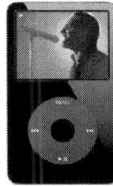

The trend is towards Flash video, not least because this is the format that YouTube currently uses. However, for delivery on Apple mobile devices (the iPod, iPhone, iPad) MP4 is the format of choice as Flash is not supported.

Video can be delivered in such a way that it can be downloaded by the user and played offline, or streamed continuously to the user with no opportunity for download. To accommodate streaming, a streaming media server is required. As an example, YouTube streams its video, whereas iTunes makes videos available for download.

Most video editing software packages will be able to export in a wide variety of compression formats.

6

A short history of online media

A short history of online media

1987

CompuServe announce the GIF graphics format, with lossless compression, transparency and animation capability. Nowhere much to use it yet, however, as no World Wide Web.

1988

The Moving Pictures Experts Group (MPEG) is established. They develop the MPEG video compression formats used primarily on CDs / DVDs but also, to a limited extent, and much later, online.

1989

Tim Berners-Lee, working at CERN, releases the first proposal for the World Wide Web. The proposal includes HTML (HyperText Markup Language), the primary basis for formatting web pages to this day.

1991

The World Wide Web is launched.

One of the first webcams was set up at Cambridge University.

The first graphical MMPORG (Massively Multiplayer Online Roleplaying Game) appears on AOL.

1992

The first SMS messages were sent from mobile phones.

1994

The first Netscape browser was launched. Support was provided for the JPEG (Joint Photographic Experts Group) format for displaying photographs online.

The first digital cameras were released.

1995

Sun Microsystems released the Java programming language, which was designed to support more sophisticated online applications than HTML could manage.

The very first VOIP (Voice Over Internet Protocol) services made it possible to communication online using voice.

The Netscape browser adds support for JavaScript, a scripting language that provides additional functionality to HTML.

1996

Microsoft acknowledge that the Internet will be a reality in the long-term and launch Internet Explorer, a free browser.

The first instant messaging systems are launched.

The PNG graphics format is launched.

RealMedia launch their audio streaming service.

Macromedia (since acquired by Adobe) launch Flash as a tool for online animation.

Microsoft launch NetMeeting, an early web conference service.

1997

RealMedia extend their streaming to include video.

The PlaceWare Auditorium web conferencing service is launched (PlaceWare has since been purchased by Microsoft).

The term 'weblog' is coined. Two years later, it is first shortened to 'blog'.

1998

The term 'webinar' is first used.

1999

Google appears.

WebEx launches its web conferencing service.

CBT Systems coins the term 'e-learning'.

2001

Launch of the Wikipedia.

Apple sells the first iPods.

2002

SecondLife introduces its online, 3D virtual world.

2003

Skype introduces internet telephony.

Apple launch iTunes as a way to download music tracks.

2004

Facebook launches.

And Flickr, as a way to share photos online.

And Firefox, a new browser, based on Netscape Navigator.

Podcasting becomes popular.

2005

YouTube allows video content to be shared online.

2006

Twitter heralds the age of micro-blogging.

2007

Apple launch the iPhone.

2010

At this point, it would be tempting to conclude that we have all of what we need in terms of tools and technologies for delivering online media. But of course we all know better than that, don't we?

... ?

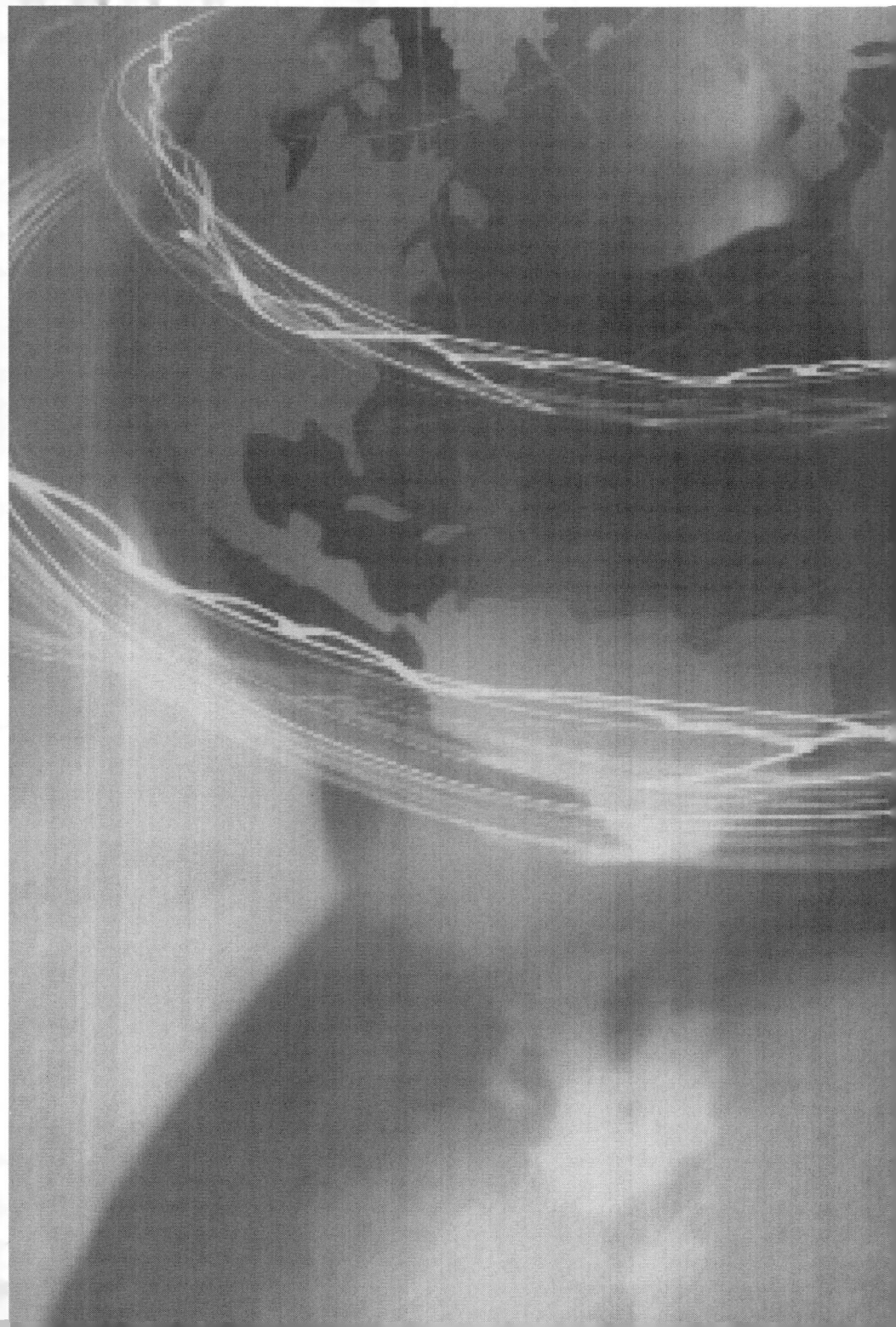